Well-being

Unlock the Power of Presence and Achieve Inner Peace with the Ultimate Guide to Mindfulness: A Transformative Journey to Enhance Your Well-Being, Boost Your Happiness and Live in the Moment

Lance P. Richards

Well-being: Unlock the Power of Presence and Achieve Inner Peace with the Ultimate Guide to Mindfulness: A Transformative Journey to Enhance Your Well-Being, Boost Your Happiness and Live in the Moment

Table of Contents

01: Introduction to Mindfulness and Well-being

Mindfulness is a practice that has been around for thousands of years, but has only recently gained widespread recognition and popularity. It is the act of bringing attention to the present moment, without judgment or distraction. Mindfulness has been shown to have a powerful impact on physical and mental well-being, and has been increasingly studied in the fields of psychology and neuroscience.

Well-being refers to the overall state of an individual's health and happiness. It encompasses many aspects of life, including physical health, emotional stability, relationships, and financial security. Achieving a state of well-being requires a holistic approach, and mindfulness can be a valuable tool for enhancing one's well-being.

Mindfulness and well-being are interconnected and complementary. By practicing mindfulness, we can become more aware of our thoughts, feelings, and bodily sensations, and develop the skills to manage them in a healthy way. This increased awareness can lead to improved physical health, reduced stress and anxiety, and increased happiness and satisfaction with life.

01: INTRODUCTION TO MINDFULNESS AND WELL-BE-ING

In this chapter, we will explore the basic principles of mindfulness and its impact on well-being. We will also look at the historical roots of mindfulness and its evolution into a modern-day practice. Finally, we will discuss the benefits of incorporating mindfulness into your life and how to get started with a mindfulness practice.

The Principles of Mindfulness

The basic principle of mindfulness is to focus on the present moment. This means becoming aware of our thoughts, feelings, and physical sensations as they happen, without judgment or distraction. Mindfulness encourages us to be curious and non-judgmental in our observations, allowing us to gain a greater understanding of our experiences.

The practice of mindfulness can be applied to any aspect of life, including daily activities such as eating, walking, and working. By bringing attention to the present moment, we can become more mindful and aware of our experiences, leading to increased well-being and happiness.

The Evolution of Mindfulness

01: INTRODUCTION TO MINDFULNESS AND WELL-BE-ING

Mindfulness has its roots in ancient Eastern traditions such as Buddhism and Taoism. It was initially developed as a spiritual practice to help individuals gain greater insight and awareness into the nature of reality. Over time, mindfulness has evolved into a secular practice that is accessible to people from all walks of life and belief systems.

In recent years, mindfulness has been increasingly studied in the fields of psychology and neuroscience. This research has provided evidence for the many benefits of mindfulness, including reduced stress and anxiety, improved physical health, and increased happiness and well-being.

Incorporating Mindfulness into Your Life

The benefits of mindfulness are numerous and well-documented. However, starting a mindfulness practice can seem overwhelming and intimidating, especially for those new to the practice. The good news is that mindfulness can be practiced in many different ways and can be tailored to fit into your individual lifestyle and schedule.

Some popular forms of mindfulness practice include meditation, yoga, tai chi, and mindfulness-based stress reduction

(MBSR) programs. These practices can be done in a group setting or individually, and can range from just a few minutes a day to several hours a week.

Incorporating mindfulness into your daily life can also be as simple as taking a few deep breaths and bringing your attention to the present moment. Paying attention to your thoughts, feelings, and physical sensations can help increase your mindfulness and overall well-being.

Conclusion

In this chapter, we have introduced the basic principles of mindfulness and its impact on well-being. We have explored the evolution of mindfulness from an ancient spiritual practice to a modern-day secular practice. Finally, we have discussed the many benefits of incorporating mindfulness into

02: Understanding the Power of Presence

Presence is a state of being fully engaged and focused in the present moment. It is the opposite of being distracted, overwhelmed, or lost in thought. When we are present, we are able to experience life with a sense of clarity and richness.

The power of presence is rooted in its ability to improve our well-being and increase our happiness. When we are present, we are able to connect with the world and our experiences in a deeper way. This connection can help reduce stress and anxiety, improve our relationships, and increase our overall sense of purpose and meaning in life.

In this chapter, we will explore the power of presence in more detail and discuss how it can be cultivated and applied in our daily lives.

The Benefits of Presence

Presence has a number of benefits that can enhance our physical and mental well-being. Some of the key benefits include:

– Reduced Stress and Anxiety: When we are present, we are

better able to manage our thoughts and emotions, reducing stress and anxiety.

– Improved Relationships: Being present in our interactions with others can help us build stronger and more meaningful relationships.

– Increased Happiness: By being present and engaged in our experiences, we can increase our overall happiness and satisfaction with life.

– Improved Focus and Productivity: Presence can help improve focus and concentration, allowing us to be more productive and effective in our work and daily activities.

– Enhanced Creativity: Presence can help us tap into our imagination and creativity, leading to increased inspiration and innovation.

Cultivating Presence

Cultivating presence is a lifelong journey and requires ongoing effort and practice. However, there are a number of practical strategies that can help you get started:

– Mindfulness Meditation: Mindfulness meditation is one

of the most effective ways to cultivate presence. By focusing on the present moment and your breath, you can learn to quiet your mind and become more present.

– Engage in Activities that You Love: Doing activities that you enjoy and find fulfilling can help you stay present and engaged in the moment.

– Practice Gratitude: Focusing on gratitude and the things you are thankful for can help you stay present and increase your overall happiness.

– Reduce Distractions: Limiting distractions, such as your phone or email, can help you stay focused and present in the moment.

– Connect with Nature: Spending time in nature can help you slow down, connect with the world around you, and become more present.

Applying Presence in Daily Life

Presence can be applied to any aspect of life, from work and relationships to leisure activities. By being present in your interactions with others and in your daily activities, you can increase your overall well-being and happiness.

For example, in your work, you can practice presence by focusing on the task at hand, reducing distractions, and being fully engaged in the moment. In your relationships, you can practice presence by listening attentively to others, being present in conversations, and showing genuine interest and empathy.

Conclusion

In this chapter, we have explored the power of presence and its impact on well-being. We have discussed the benefits of presence, including reduced stress and anxiety, improved relationships, increased happiness, and enhanced creativity. We have also looked at strategies for cultivating presence and how it can be applied to our daily lives. By practicing presence, we can live in the moment, connect with our experiences, and enhance our overall well-being.

03: The Benefits of Mindfulness for Your Well-being

Mindfulness is the practice of being present and fully engaged in the moment. It involves paying attention to your thoughts, feelings, and physical sensations, without judgment or distraction. Over the past few decades, mindfulness has been extensively researched and has been shown to have numerous benefits for mental and physical health.

In this chapter, we will explore the benefits of mindfulness for well-being and how it can be incorporated into your daily life to enhance your overall happiness and quality of life.

Reduces Stress and Anxiety

One of the most well-known benefits of mindfulness is its ability to reduce stress and anxiety. By paying attention to the present moment, we can distance ourselves from negative thoughts and feelings, and learn to manage them in a more effective way. This can help reduce feelings of anxiety and stress and improve our overall mental health.

Improves Emotional Regulation

Mindfulness can also help improve emotional regulation, by enabling us to become more aware of our emotions and respond to them in a healthier way. When we are mindful, we are better equipped to recognize when we are feeling overwhelmed or upset, and can take steps to regulate our emotions and regain our composure.

Enhances Concentration and Productivity

Mindfulness can also help improve concentration and productivity. When we are mindful, we are better able to stay focused and engaged in the present moment, reducing distractions and increasing our ability to perform tasks more efficiently.

Boosts Immune System

Studies have shown that mindfulness can also have a positive impact on physical health. It has been found to boost the immune system, reduce chronic pain, and improve sleep. By reducing stress and anxiety, mindfulness can also help lower the risk of developing certain health conditions, such as heart disease and stroke.

03: THE BENEFITS OF MINDFULNESS FOR YOUR WELL-BEING

Improves Relationships

Mindfulness can also have a positive impact on relationships. By being present in our interactions with others and paying attention to our thoughts and feelings, we can become more compassionate and empathetic, improving our connections with others and building stronger, more meaningful relationships.

Incorporating Mindfulness into Daily Life

Incorporating mindfulness into your daily life can be as simple as taking a few minutes each day to be present and mindful. This can be done through activities such as mindfulness meditation, yoga, or simply paying attention to your breath and the sensations in your body.

It is also important to be mindful in your interactions with others, by actively listening, being present in conversations, and showing genuine interest and empathy.

In addition, incorporating mindfulness into your work and leisure activities can help you stay present and focused, leading to increased productivity and enjoyment.

Conclusion

In this chapter, we have explored the benefits of mindfulness for well-being, including reduced stress and anxiety, improved emotional regulation, enhanced concentration and productivity, improved relationships, and a boost to the immune system. By incorporating mindfulness into your daily life, you can improve your overall happiness and well-being, and live a more fulfilling life.

04: How to Incorporate Mindfulness into Your Daily Life

Mindfulness is a powerful tool that can help enhance your well-being and improve your quality of life. However, making mindfulness a part of your daily routine can seem like a daunting task. In this chapter, we will explore practical tips and strategies to help you incorporate mindfulness into your daily life and make it a habit.

Start Small

The first step in incorporating mindfulness into your daily life is to start small. You do not need to set aside hours each day to practice mindfulness. Instead, start with just a few minutes each day, and gradually increase the amount of time you spend being mindful as you become more comfortable with the practice.

Find Your Own Mindfulness Practice

There is no one right way to practice mindfulness. It is important to find what works best for you, whether that be meditation, yoga, walking, or another mindfulness exercise. Experiment with different mindfulness techniques and find the one that resonates with you the most.

Make Time for Mindfulness

Incorporating mindfulness into your daily life requires making time for it. This can mean setting aside specific times each day for mindfulness practices, such as first thing in the morning or last thing at night. It can also mean making mindfulness a part of your daily routines, such as taking a mindful walk after dinner or taking a few mindful breaths before starting a new task.

Incorporate Mindfulness into Your Work and Leisure Activities

Mindfulness is not just about dedicated mindfulness practices. It is also about being present and mindful in your daily activities. This can involve paying attention to the present moment while cooking, gardening, or even doing household chores. You can also incorporate mindfulness into your work by being present in meetings and taking regular breaks to check in with yourself and your thoughts and feelings.

04: HOW TO INCORPORATE MINDFULNESS INTO YOUR DAILY LIFE

Make Mindfulness a Priority

Incorporating mindfulness into your daily life requires making it a priority. This means setting aside distractions, such as phones and other electronic devices, and being fully present in the moment. It also means letting go of perfectionism and not getting too caught up in the outcome of your mindfulness practice.

Enlist the Help of Others

Finally, incorporating mindfulness into your daily life can be made easier with the support of others. You can join a mindfulness group, work with a mindfulness coach, or practice with a friend. Having someone to share your mindfulness journey with can provide encouragement, accountability, and motivation to continue incorporating mindfulness into your daily life.

Conclusion

Incorporating mindfulness into your daily life can be a transformative experience, leading to improved well-being, enhanced happiness, and a greater sense of inner peace. By

starting small, finding your own mindfulness practice, making time for mindfulness, incorporating mindfulness into
your work and leisure activities, making mindfulness a priority, and enlisting the help of others, you can make mindfulness a habit and reap its many benefits.

05: The Science of Mindfulness and Its Impact on the Brain

In recent years, mindfulness has become a popular topic in the field of psychology and neuroscience. Researchers have studied the impact of mindfulness on the brain, and the results are clear: mindfulness can have a positive impact on mental and physical health. In this chapter, we will explore the science of mindfulness and its impact on the brain.

The Definition of Mindfulness

Mindfulness is often defined as the practice of being fully present and engaged in the moment, without judgment. This means paying attention to our thoughts, feelings, and sensations without getting caught up in them. Mindfulness has been practiced for thousands of years in various spiritual and religious traditions, but it is only in recent years that researchers have begun to study its impact on the brain and mental health.

The Brain and Mindfulness

Research has shown that mindfulness has a positive impact on the brain. When we practice mindfulness, we activate the parts of the brain responsible for regulating attention, emotions, and thoughts. This can help us regulate our emotions, reduce stress and anxiety, and improve our overall well-being.

One of the ways in which mindfulness can impact the brain is by increasing activity in the prefrontal cortex, the part of the brain responsible for attention and executive function. Research has shown that mindfulness can improve our ability to focus, reduce distractions, and increase our ability to switch between tasks.

Another way in which mindfulness can impact the brain is by reducing activity in the amygdala, the part of the brain responsible for regulating emotions. This can help reduce stress, anxiety, and depression, and improve our overall emotional well-being.

Finally, mindfulness can impact the brain by increasing the production of neurotransmitters such as dopamine, serotonin, and norepinephrine. These neurotransmitters are responsible for regulating mood, motivation, and attention, and increasing their levels can help improve our overall mental and physical health.

05: THE SCIENCE OF MINDFULNESS AND ITS IMPACT ON THE BRAIN

The Impact of Mindfulness on Mental Health

In addition to its impact on the brain, mindfulness can also have a positive impact on mental health. Research has shown that mindfulness can reduce symptoms of anxiety and depression, improve our ability to cope with stress, and increase overall well-being.

Mindfulness can also help us build resilience, allowing us to bounce back from challenges and setbacks. This is because mindfulness helps us develop a non-judgmental attitude towards our thoughts and feelings, allowing us to respond to stress and adversity in a more effective and healthy way.

The Impact of Mindfulness on Physical Health

Mindfulness can also have a positive impact on physical health. Research has shown that mindfulness can help reduce chronic pain, improve sleep, and even boost the immune system.

In addition, mindfulness has been shown to help people with chronic conditions, such as heart disease, diabetes, and cancer, better manage their symptoms and improve their quality of life.

Conclusion

The science of mindfulness and its impact on the brain is a
growing area of research, but the results are clear: mindfulness can have a positive impact on mental and physical
health. Whether it be reducing stress and anxiety, improving our ability to cope with adversity, or improving physical
health, mindfulness is a powerful tool that can help us
achieve greater well-being and live a happier and more fulfilling life.

06: Mindful Breathing Techniques for Inner Peace

Breathing is an essential part of life, but it is often something that we take for granted. However, the way we breathe can have a profound impact on our mental and physical well-being. That's why mindful breathing techniques are an important aspect of mindfulness practice. In this chapter, we will explore some of the most effective breathing techniques for inner peace and how you can incorporate them into your daily life.

The Basics of Mindful Breathing

Mindful breathing is the practice of paying attention to your breath as it moves in and out of your body. It is a simple but powerful tool that can help you achieve inner peace and reduce stress and anxiety.

When we are stressed or anxious, our breathing becomes shallow and rapid. This can cause our heart rate to increase, leading to further stress and anxiety. However, by focusing on our breath and slowing it down, we can reduce the physical symptoms of stress and anxiety and achieve a greater sense of calm and relaxation.

06: MINDFUL BREATHING TECHNIQUES FOR INNER PEACE

Mindful Breathing Techniques

– The 4-7-8 Breathing Technique: This technique involves breathing in for four counts, holding your breath for seven counts, and exhaling for eight counts. Repeat this pattern several times and focus on your breath as you do so.

– Box Breathing: This technique involves breathing in for four counts, holding your breath for four counts, breathing out for four counts, and then holding your breath for four counts before starting the cycle again.

– The Belly Breath: This technique involves focusing on the movement of your belly as you breathe in and out. Place one hand on your belly and breathe in deeply, feeling your hand rise. Then, exhale slowly, feeling your hand fall. Repeat this several times, focusing on your breath and the movement of your belly.

– The Alternate Nostril Breathing: This technique involves breathing in through one nostril and out through the other, alternating sides with each breath. This technique can help balance the right and left sides of the brain, promoting relaxation and inner peace.

06: MINDFUL BREATHING TECHNIQUES FOR INNER PEACE

Incorporating Mindful Breathing into Your Daily Life

One of the great things about mindful breathing is that it can be done anywhere, at any time. You can practice mindful breathing while sitting at your desk, waiting in line, or even while lying in bed.

It is important to make mindful breathing a part of your daily routine. Set aside a few minutes each day to practice mindful breathing and gradually increase the amount of time you spend on it as you get more comfortable with the technique.

Conclusion

Mindful breathing is a simple but powerful tool that can help you achieve inner peace and reduce stress and anxiety. Whether you are new to mindfulness or have been practicing for a while, incorporating mindful breathing techniques into your daily routine can have a profound impact on your mental and physical well-being. So take a deep breath, focus on your breath, and start your journey towards inner peace and greater well-being.

07: Understanding Your Thoughts and Emotions through Mindfulness

One of the key benefits of mindfulness is its ability to help us understand and manage our thoughts and emotions. Our thoughts and emotions can have a significant impact on our mental and physical well-being, and often, we can become overwhelmed by them. However, by practicing mindfulness, we can gain a greater awareness of our thoughts and emotions, allowing us to respond to them in a more positive and productive manner.

The Nature of Thoughts and Emotions

Thoughts and emotions are an integral part of our lives, and they are always present, even if we are not aware of them. Our thoughts can be positive, negative, or neutral, and they can range from the practical and rational to the irrational and exaggerated. Our emotions, on the other hand, are complex and can be difficult to understand. They can range from joy and happiness to sadness and anger, and they can be triggered by our thoughts, experiences, and the people and events in our lives.

07: UNDERSTANDING YOUR THOUGHTS AND EMOTIONS THROUGH MINDFULNESS

The Benefits of Understanding Your Thoughts and Emotions through Mindfulness

By practicing mindfulness, we can become more aware of our thoughts and emotions, allowing us to respond to them in a more positive and productive manner. This can help us reduce stress and anxiety, improve our relationships with others, and increase our overall sense of well-being.

For example, when we are mindful, we can observe our thoughts and emotions without judgment, allowing us to respond to them in a more effective manner. This can help us avoid becoming overwhelmed by negative thoughts and emotions, and instead, we can take a more proactive approach to managing them.

Mindfulness Techniques for Understanding Your Thoughts and Emotions

– The Body Scan: This technique involves focusing on each part of your body, starting from the top of your head and moving down to your toes. As you do so, pay attention to any thoughts and emotions that arise, and observe them without judgment.

07: UNDERSTANDING YOUR THOUGHTS AND EMO- TIONS THROUGH MINDFULNESS

– The Mindful Walk: This technique involves taking a walk and focusing on each step as you take it. Pay attention to your thoughts and emotions as they arise, and observe them without judgment.

– The Body Check-In: This technique involves taking a moment to check in with your body, paying attention to any physical sensations or emotions that may be present. Observe these sensations and emotions without judgment, and focus on your breath as you do so.

– The Thought Watch: This technique involves observing your thoughts as they arise, without getting caught up in them. Imagine that you are watching your thoughts from a distance, and observe them without judgment.

Incorporating Mindfulness into Your Daily Life

It is important to make mindfulness a part of your daily routine. Start by setting aside a few minutes each day to practice mindfulness and gradually increase the amount of time you spend on it as you get more comfortable with the techniques.

07: UNDERSTANDING YOUR THOUGHTS AND EMOTIONS THROUGH MINDFULNESS

You can also incorporate mindfulness into your daily life by paying attention to your thoughts and emotions throughout the day. Whenever you notice that you are getting caught up in your thoughts or emotions, take a moment to pause and observe them without judgment. Focus on your breath and the sensations in your body, and try to remain present in the moment.

Conclusion

By practicing mindfulness, we can become more aware of our thoughts and emotions, allowing us to respond to them in a more positive and productive manner. Whether you are new to mindfulness or have been practicing for a while, incorporating mindfulness into your daily life can help you reduce stress and anxiety, improve your relationships with others, and increase your overall sense of well-being. So start your journey towards greater understanding and mastery of your thoughts and emotions today.

08: How to Use Mindfulness to Overcome Stress and Anxiety

Stress and anxiety are common experiences that affect many people. They can cause physical and emotional symptoms that can interfere with our daily lives and impact our overall well-being. However, by incorporating mindfulness into our daily routine, we can learn how to manage stress and anxiety in a more positive and productive manner.

What is Stress and Anxiety?

Stress is a natural response to a challenging or demanding situation, and it is an inevitable part of life. It is a physiological response that prepares our body to respond to a threat or challenge. However, when stress becomes chronic, it can have negative effects on our health and well-being.

Anxiety is a feeling of unease, such as worry or fear, that can range from mild to severe. It is a normal part of life, and it can be a healthy response to certain situations, such as public speaking or taking a test. However, when anxiety becomes chronic and interferes with our daily lives, it can be classified as an anxiety disorder.

08: HOW TO USE MINDFULNESS TO OVERCOME STRESS AND ANXIETY

The Benefits of Mindfulness for Stress and Anxiety

Mindfulness has been shown to be an effective tool for reducing stress and anxiety. By practicing mindfulness, we can become more aware of our thoughts and emotions, allowing us to respond to them in a more positive and productive manner. This can help us reduce stress and anxiety, improve our relationships with others, and increase our overall sense of well-being.

For example, when we are mindful, we can observe our thoughts and emotions without judgment, allowing us to respond to them in a more effective manner. This can help us avoid becoming overwhelmed by negative thoughts and emotions, and instead, we can take a more proactive approach to managing them.

Mindfulness Techniques for Overcoming Stress and Anxiety

– The Body Scan: This technique involves focusing on each part of your body, starting from the top of your head and moving down to your toes. As you do so, pay attention to any thoughts and emotions that arise, and observe them without judgment.

08: HOW TO USE MINDFULNESS TO OVERCOME STRESS AND ANXIETY

– The Mindful Walk: This technique involves taking a walk and focusing on each step as you take it. Pay attention to your thoughts and emotions as they arise, and observe them without judgment.

– The Body Check-In: This technique involves taking a moment to check in with your body, paying attention to any physical sensations or emotions that may be present. Observe these sensations and emotions without judgment, and focus on your breath as you do so.

– The Thought Watch: This technique involves observing your thoughts as they arise, without getting caught up in them. Imagine that you are watching your thoughts from a distance, and observe them without judgment.

Incorporating Mindfulness into Your Daily Life

It is important to make mindfulness a part of your daily routine. Start by setting aside a few minutes each day to practice mindfulness and gradually increase the amount of time you spend on it as you get more comfortable with the techniques.

08: HOW TO USE MINDFULNESS TO OVERCOME STRESS AND ANXIETY

You can also incorporate mindfulness into your daily life by paying attention to your thoughts and emotions throughout the day. Whenever you notice that you are getting caught up in your thoughts or emotions, take a moment to pause and observe them without judgment. Focus on your breath and the sensations in your body, and try to remain present in the moment.

Conclusion

By incorporating mindfulness into your daily routine, you can learn how to manage stress and anxiety in a more positive and productive manner. Whether you are new to mindfulness or have been practicing for a while, making mindfulness a part of your daily life can help you reduce stress and anxiety, improve your relationships with others, and increase your overall sense of well

09: Mindful Movement: The Benefits of Yoga, Meditation and Tai Chi

Incorporating mindful movement into your daily routine can have a positive impact on your physical and mental well-being. Whether you prefer yoga, meditation, or Tai Chi, these practices can help you develop a deeper connection with your body, mind, and spirit. They can also help you reduce stress, improve your focus and concentration, and boost your overall sense of well-being.

What is Yoga?

Yoga is a physical and mental practice that originated in ancient India. It involves a combination of physical postures, breathing techniques, and meditation. The goal of yoga is to promote physical and mental well-being and help practitioners develop a deeper connection with their body, mind, and spirit.

The Benefits of Yoga

Yoga has been shown to have numerous benefits for physical and mental well-being. These include:

09: MINDFUL MOVEMENT: THE BENEFITS OF YOGA, MEDITATION AND TAI CHI

– Improved flexibility and strength

– Reduced stress and anxiety

– Improved sleep

– Better focus and concentration

– Increased energy levels

What is Meditation?

Meditation is a mental practice that involves focusing the mind on a particular object, sound, breath, or other point of focus. The goal of meditation is to help practitioners develop a deeper sense of awareness and connection with their mind and body.

The Benefits of Meditation

Meditation has been shown to have numerous benefits for physical and mental well-being. These include:

– Reduced stress and anxiety

– Improved focus and concentration

09: MINDFUL MOVEMENT: THE BENEFITS OF YOGA, MEDITATION AND TAI CHI

– Increased feelings of happiness and well-being

– Improved sleep

– Better management of chronic pain

What is Tai Chi?

Tai Chi is a Chinese martial art that involves slow, flowing movements, deep breathing, and visualization. The practice originated in China as a form of self-defense, but it has since evolved into a form of exercise and meditation. The goal of Tai Chi is to promote physical and mental well-being and help practitioners develop a deeper connection with their body, mind, and spirit.

The Benefits of Tai Chi

Tai Chi has been shown to have numerous benefits for physical and mental well-being. These include:

– Improved balance and coordination

– Reduced stress and anxiety

– Improved focus and concentration

09: MINDFUL MOVEMENT: THE BENEFITS OF YOGA, MEDITATION AND TAI CHI

– Increased energy levels

– Better management of chronic pain

Incorporating Mindful Movement into Your Daily Life

To get the most out of yoga, meditation, or Tai Chi, it is important to incorporate these practices into your daily routine. Start by setting aside a few minutes each day to practice, and gradually increase the amount of time you spend on it as you get more comfortable with the techniques.

You can also incorporate mindful movement into your daily life by paying attention to your body and movements throughout the day. Whether you are walking, running, or simply sitting at your desk, try to remain mindful and present in the moment, paying attention to your breath and the sensations in your body.

Conclusion

Incorporating mindful movement into your daily routine, such as yoga, meditation, or Tai Chi, can have a positive impact on your physical and mental well-being. Whether you are new to these practices or have been doing them for a while, making them a part of your daily life can help you reduce stress, improve your focus and concentration, and boost your overall sense of well-being.

10: The Art of Mindful Communication

Mindful communication is the practice of being fully present and attentive in all of your interactions with others. It involves paying attention to your thoughts, feelings, and sensations in the moment, as well as those of the people you are communicating with. When you engage in mindful communication, you are able to connect with others on a deeper level, build stronger relationships, and reduce conflicts and misunderstandings.

Why is Mindful Communication Important?

Mindful communication is important because it can have a positive impact on your relationships and overall well-being. When you engage in mindful communication, you are able to connect with others on a deeper level, build stronger relationships, and reduce conflicts and misunderstandings.

In addition, mindful communication can help you to become more self-aware, improve your emotional intelligence, and enhance your ability to navigate difficult conversations and interactions. By developing your ability to communicate mindfully, you can become a more effective communicator and build stronger, healthier relationships with others.

The Elements of Mindful Communication

Mindful communication involves several key elements, including:

– Presence: Being fully present and attentive in the moment, paying attention to your thoughts, feelings, and sensations, as well as those of the person you are communicating with.

– Listening: Focusing your attention on what the other person is saying, without interrupting or allowing your mind to wander.

– Empathy: Understanding the thoughts, feelings, and perspectives of the other person, and expressing empathy and understanding.

– Authenticity: Being honest and open in your interactions, sharing your thoughts and feelings without hiding behind a mask.

– Respect: Treating the other person with respect and dignity, regardless of your differences or disagreements.

10: THE ART OF MINDFUL COMMUNICATION

Tips for Improving Your Mindful Communication Skills

There are several steps you can take to improve your mindful communication skills, including:

— Practice mindfulness: To become a more effective communicator, it is important to practice mindfulness in your daily life. This can help you to become more self-aware, develop greater emotional intelligence, and enhance your ability to connect with others.

— Listen actively: When you are communicating with others, make a conscious effort to focus your attention on what they are saying. Avoid interrupting or allowing your mind to wander, and try to understand their perspective.

— Speak authentically: When you are communicating, be honest and open about your thoughts and feelings. Avoid hiding behind a mask, and be authentic in your interactions with others.

— Show empathy: Try to understand the thoughts, feelings, and perspectives of the other person, and express empathy and understanding.

– Practice active listening: Make a conscious effort to listen to the other person, and avoid interrupting or allowing your mind to wander.

– Be respectful: Treat the other person with respect and dignity, regardless of your differences or disagreements.

Conclusion

Mindful communication is the practice of being fully present and attentive in all of your interactions with others. By incorporating the elements of presence, listening, empathy, authenticity, and respect, you can improve your mindful communication skills, connect with others on a deeper level, and build stronger, healthier relationships. Whether you are communicating with friends, family, or coworkers, mindful communication can help you to navigate difficult conversations, reduce conflicts and misunderstandings, and become a more effective communicator.

11: Mindful Eating: A Guide to Nourishing Your Body and Mind

Mindful eating is the practice of being fully present and attentive while eating, paying attention to the experience of eating and savoring the flavors, textures, and aromas of your food. It involves making a conscious effort to slow down and enjoy your food, rather than mindlessly eating while distracted.

Why is Mindful Eating Important?

Mindful eating is important because it can have a positive impact on your physical and emotional health. When you engage in mindful eating, you are able to better tune into your body's hunger and fullness cues, which can help you to make healthier food choices and avoid overeating.

In addition, mindful eating can help you to reduce stress and improve your overall well-being. By making a conscious effort to savor and enjoy your food, you can become more aware of your body's sensations and develop a deeper appreciation for the nourishing effects of food.

The Benefits of Mindful Eating

11: MINDFUL EATING: A GUIDE TO NOURISHING YOUR BODY AND MIND

There are several key benefits to engaging in mindful eating, including:

– Improved physical health: By tuning into your body's hunger and fullness cues, you can make healthier food choices and avoid overeating, which can have a positive impact on your physical health.

– Enhanced emotional well-being: Mindful eating can help you to reduce stress and improve your overall well-being by allowing you to savor and enjoy your food.

– Better digestion: When you eat mindfully, you are able to chew your food more thoroughly, which can improve your digestion and reduce digestive discomfort.

– Increased awareness: Mindful eating helps you to become more aware of your body's sensations and develop a deeper appreciation for the nourishing effects of food.

Tips for Mindful Eating

There are several steps you can take to engage in mindful eating, including:

11: MINDFUL EATING: A GUIDE TO NOURISHING YOUR BODY AND MIND

– Slow down: Make a conscious effort to slow down and savor your food, rather than eating mindlessly while distracted.

– Pay attention to your food: Pay attention to the colors, flavors, textures, and aromas of your food, and enjoy the experience of eating.

– Chew your food thoroughly: Take the time to chew your food thoroughly, which can improve your digestion and help you to enjoy your food more.

– Tune into your body's hunger and fullness cues: Pay attention to your body's hunger and fullness cues, and eat until you are satisfied, but not stuffed.

– Avoid distractions: Avoid eating while distracted, such as while watching TV or working at your computer.

– Be present: Be fully present and attentive while eating, and focus on the experience of eating and savoring your food.

Conclusion

11: MINDFUL EATING: A GUIDE TO NOURISHING YOUR BODY AND MIND

Mindful eating is the practice of being fully present and attentive while eating, paying attention to the experience of eating and savoring the flavors, textures, and aromas of your food. By incorporating the tips for mindful eating, you can improve your physical and emotional health, reduce stress, and enjoy your food more. Whether you are eating alone or with others, mindful eating can help you to develop a deeper appreciation for the nourishing effects of food, and become more aware of your body's sensations.

12: The Power of Nature: Connecting with the Outdoors for Mindful Living

Nature has a profound impact on our well-being, and spending time in nature can be a powerful way to cultivate mindfulness and inner peace. When we connect with nature, we are able to tune out the distractions and demands of everyday life, and focus instead on the present moment and the beauty of the natural world around us.

Why is Nature Important for Mindful Living?

Nature has a calming and rejuvenating effect on our mind and body, and has been shown to have numerous health benefits. Spending time in nature has been linked to reduced stress levels, improved mental clarity, and increased feelings of happiness and well-being.

In addition, connecting with nature can help us to cultivate mindfulness and live in the moment. When we are surrounded by the beauty and serenity of nature, we are able to focus on the present moment and become more mindful of our thoughts, feelings, and physical sensations.

12: THE POWER OF NATURE: CONNECTING WITH THE OUTDOORS FOR MINDFUL LIVING

The Benefits of Connecting with Nature

There are several key benefits to connecting with nature, including:

– Reduced stress levels: Spending time in nature has been linked to reduced stress levels, as it provides a calming and rejuvenating escape from the demands of everyday life.

– Improved mental clarity: Connecting with nature can help to clear your mind and improve mental clarity, as you focus on the present moment and the beauty of the natural world around you.

– Increased happiness: Spending time in nature has been linked to increased feelings of happiness and well-being, as it provides a sense of peace and serenity.

– Cultivation of mindfulness: Connecting with nature helps to cultivate mindfulness and live in the moment, as you focus on the present moment and become more mindful of your thoughts, feelings, and physical sensations.

Tips for Connecting with Nature

12: THE POWER OF NATURE: CONNECTING WITH THE OUTDOORS FOR MINDFUL LIVING

There are several steps you can take to connect with nature and incorporate it into your daily life, including:

– Get outside: Spend time in nature every day, even if it is just for a few minutes. Go for a walk in a park, sit by a lake, or simply enjoy the view from your window.

– Disconnect from technology: Disconnect from technology and put away your phone, laptop, and other distractions when you are outside in nature.

– Pay attention to your senses: Pay attention to the sounds, sights, and smells of nature, and savor the experience of being outside.

– Practice mindfulness: Use nature as an opportunity to practice mindfulness and live in the moment, focusing on your thoughts, feelings, and physical sensations.

– Connect with nature in new ways: Explore new ways to connect with nature, such as hiking, camping, or bird-watching.

Conclusion

12: THE POWER OF NATURE: CONNECTING WITH THE OUTDOORS FOR MINDFUL LIVING

Nature has a profound impact on our well-being, and connecting with nature can be a powerful way to cultivate mindfulness and inner peace. By spending time in nature and focusing on the present moment, we are able to reduce stress, improve mental clarity, and increase feelings of happiness and well-being. Whether you are spending time in a park, a forest, or simply looking out your window, connecting with nature is an essential part of a mindful and fulfilling life.

13: How to Cultivate Gratitude and Positive Thinking through Mindfulness

Gratitude and positive thinking are powerful tools for improving our mental and emotional well-being, and can be cultivated through the practice of mindfulness. When we are able to focus on the present moment and be grateful for what we have, we are better able to overcome stress, anxiety, and negative thoughts.

The Benefits of Gratitude and Positive Thinking

There are several key benefits to cultivating gratitude and positive thinking, including:

– Improved mood: Gratitude has been linked to improved mood and increased feelings of happiness, as it helps to shift our focus from what we lack to what we have.

– Increased resilience: Positive thinking has been shown to increase resilience and help us to better cope with stress, anxiety, and negative thoughts.

– Improved relationships: When we are able to focus on

gratitude and the positive aspects of our lives, we are better able to form and maintain healthy relationships with others.

– Improved physical health: Positive thinking has been linked to improved physical health, including reduced stress levels and a stronger immune system.

How to Cultivate Gratitude and Positive Thinking through Mindfulness

There are several steps you can take to cultivate gratitude and positive thinking through mindfulness, including:

– Practice mindfulness: The foundation of cultivating gratitude and positive thinking is the practice of mindfulness, as it helps us to focus on the present moment and become more aware of our thoughts and feelings.

– Keep a gratitude journal: Write down three things you are grateful for each day, as this can help to shift your focus from what you lack to what you have.

– Practice positive affirmations: Repeat positive affirmations to yourself each day, such as "I am worthy," "I am enough," or "I am capable."

13: HOW TO CULTIVATE GRATITUDE AND POSITIVE THINKING THROUGH MINDFULNESS

– Focus on the present moment: When you are feeling stressed or overwhelmed, focus on the present moment and the things you have in your life, rather than dwelling on the past or worrying about the future.

– Surround yourself with positivity: Surround yourself with positive people and things, such as books, music, or images that inspire and uplift you.

Conclusion

Gratitude and positive thinking are powerful tools for improving our mental and emotional well-being, and can be cultivated through the practice of mindfulness. By focusing on the present moment and being grateful for what we have, we are better able to overcome stress, anxiety, and negative thoughts, and live a more fulfilling and meaningful life. Whether through journaling, positive affirmations, or simply focusing on the present moment, incorporating gratitude and positive thinking into your mindfulness practice can help you to live a happier, healthier, and more fulfilled life.

14: Mindful Parenting: Raising Children with Compassion and Understanding

Parenting can be a challenging and rewarding experience, but it can also be stressful and overwhelming. By incorporating mindfulness into our parenting approach, we can cultivate more compassion and understanding for ourselves and our children, leading to improved relationships and better outcomes for everyone involved.

The Benefits of Mindful Parenting

There are several key benefits to practicing mindful parenting, including:

– Improved relationships: By being more present and attentive to our children's needs and emotions, we can build stronger and more positive relationships with them.

– Increased empathy: Mindful parenting can help us to better understand our children's perspectives and feelings, leading to increased empathy and compassion for them.

– Decreased stress: Mindful parenting can help us to better

manage our own stress and emotions, leading to a more peaceful and harmonious household.

– Improved communication: By being more attentive and present, we can improve our communication skills and better understand our children's needs and wants.

How to Incorporate Mindfulness into Your Parenting

There are several steps you can take to incorporate mindfulness into your parenting approach, including:

– Practice mindfulness: The foundation of mindful parenting is the practice of mindfulness, so make sure to take time each day to focus on your breath, become more aware of your thoughts and emotions, and cultivate a sense of calm and peace.

– Pay attention to your child's needs: Take time to listen to your child and understand their needs and feelings, without judgment or distraction.

– Speak kindly: Use positive and uplifting language when speaking to your child, and avoid criticism or negativity.

14: MINDFUL PARENTING: RAISING CHILDREN WITH COMPASSION AND UNDERSTANDING

– Lead by example: Model the behavior you want to see in your child, and be mindful of the words and actions you use.

– Find joy in the moment: Rather than focusing on the past or worrying about the future, find joy and happiness in the present moment and the things you can do together as a family.

Conclusion

Parenting can be a challenging and rewarding experience, but it can also be stressful and overwhelming. By incorporating mindfulness into our parenting approach, we can cultivate more compassion and understanding for ourselves and our children, leading to improved relationships and better outcomes for everyone involved. Whether through focusing on your breath, paying attention to your child's needs, or simply finding joy in the moment, incorporating mindfulness into your parenting approach can help you to raise children with kindness, empathy, and understanding, and lead a more fulfilling and meaningful life.

15: Mindful Leadership: Building Strong Relationships and Empowering Teams

Leadership is about guiding and inspiring others towards a common goal, and mindfulness can play a key role in this process. By incorporating mindfulness into our leadership style, we can cultivate better relationships, improve our decision-making skills, and empower our teams to achieve their full potential.

The Benefits of Mindful Leadership

There are several key benefits to practicing mindful leadership, including:

– Improved decision-making: Mindfulness can help leaders to slow down, gather information, and make more informed and effective decisions.

– Stronger relationships: Mindful leaders are better able to understand their team members' needs and perspectives, leading to improved relationships and better collaboration.

– Increased empathy: Mindfulness can help leaders to better understand the emotions and motivations of their team members, leading to increased empathy and compassion.

– Decreased stress: Mindful leaders are better able to manage their own stress and emotions, leading to a more peaceful and harmonious work environment.

How to Incorporate Mindfulness into Your Leadership

There are several steps you can take to incorporate mindfulness into your leadership approach, including:

– Practice mindfulness: Make sure to take time each day to focus on your breath, become more aware of your thoughts and emotions, and cultivate a sense of calm and peace.

– Listen actively: Take time to listen to your team members, without judgment or distraction, and understand their needs and perspectives.

– Communicate clearly: Use clear and concise language when communicating with your team, and avoid confusion or misunderstandings.

– Lead by example: Model the behavior you want to see in

your team, and be mindful of the words and actions you use.

– Encourage growth: Foster an environment of growth and development, where team members feel empowered to learn, grow, and succeed.

Conclusion

Mindful leadership is about inspiring and guiding others towards a common goal, while building strong relationships and empowering teams to achieve their full potential. By incorporating mindfulness into your leadership style, you can improve your decision-making skills, better understand your team members' needs and perspectives, and cultivate a more peaceful and harmonious work environment. Whether through focused breathing, active listening, or encouraging growth, incorporating mindfulness into your leadership approach can help you to become a more effective and empathetic leader, and lead your team to success.

16: Mindful Relationships: The Power of Connection and Communication

Relationships are a key aspect of our lives, and mindfulness can play a vital role in helping us to create and maintain strong, fulfilling connections with others. Whether it's with a romantic partner, family members, friends, or colleagues, mindfulness can help us to cultivate deeper understanding, greater empathy, and more effective communication, leading to stronger and more satisfying relationships.

The Benefits of Mindful Relationships

There are several key benefits to practicing mindfulness in our relationships, including:

– Improved communication: Mindfulness can help us to become better listeners, and to express ourselves in a clear, non-judgmental, and empathetic way, leading to more effective and meaningful communication.

– Increased empathy: By being more aware of our thoughts and emotions, as well as those of others, mindfulness can help us to better understand the motivations and perspectives of those we care about.

— Stronger bonds: By cultivating deeper understanding and empathy, mindfulness can help us to create stronger and more fulfilling connections with others.

— Decreased conflict: Mindful relationships are less likely to experience conflict, as we are better able to understand and manage our own emotions and those of others.

How to Incorporate Mindfulness into Your Relationships

There are several steps you can take to incorporate mindfulness into your relationships, including:

— Practice mindfulness: Take time each day to focus on your breath, become more aware of your thoughts and emotions, and cultivate a sense of calm and peace.

— Listen actively: Take time to listen to your loved ones, without judgment or distraction, and understand their needs and perspectives.

— Communicate clearly: Use clear and concise language when communicating with those you care about, and avoid confusion or misunderstandings.

– Cultivate empathy: Try to understand the emotions and motivations of others, and be compassionate and understanding in your interactions.

– Foster connection: Make time for activities and experiences that bring you and your loved ones closer together, and create shared memories and connections.

Conclusion

Mindful relationships are about fostering deeper understanding, greater empathy, and more effective communication, leading to stronger and more fulfilling connections with others. Whether through active listening, clear communication, or cultivating empathy, incorporating mindfulness into our relationships can help us to create more meaningful and satisfying connections with the people who matter most to us. By prioritizing mindfulness in our relationships, we can deepen our bonds, reduce conflict, and create a more peaceful and harmonious environment for everyone involved.

17: Mindful Aging: Embracing Life with Wisdom and Joy

Aging can be a time of great change and transformation, and mindfulness can play a vital role in helping us to navigate this time with grace, wisdom, and joy. By cultivating awareness and acceptance of the present moment, we can learn to embrace the aging process and find meaning, purpose, and joy in the journey.

The Benefits of Mindful Aging

There are several key benefits to practicing mindfulness as we age, including:

– Increased self-awareness: Mindfulness can help us to become more aware of our thoughts, emotions, and physical sensations, leading to greater self-awareness and insight.

– Reduced stress and anxiety: By becoming more mindful of the present moment, we can learn to manage stress and anxiety, and find peace and calm in the face of life's challenges.

– Improved physical health: Mindfulness has been shown to have numerous health benefits, including reduced inflammation, improved sleep, and a stronger immune system.

– Increased emotional resilience: By cultivating a sense of calm and peace, mindfulness can help us to become more resilient in the face of life's ups and downs.

– A greater sense of purpose: As we age, mindfulness can help us to find meaning and purpose in our lives, and to live with greater intention and purpose.

How to Incorporate Mindfulness into Your Aging Journey

There are several steps you can take to incorporate mindfulness into your aging journey, including:

– Practice mindfulness regularly: Take time each day to focus on your breath, become more aware of your thoughts and emotions, and cultivate a sense of calm and peace.

– Embrace change: Accept that change is a natural part of aging, and embrace each new stage of life with openness and curiosity.

– Cultivate gratitude: Practice gratitude and appreciate the simple pleasures of life, finding joy in the moment and contentment in what you have.

– Engage in physical activity: Participate in physical activity, such as yoga or tai chi, to improve physical health and well-being.

– Nourish your mind and body: Take care of your body and mind, eating a balanced diet, getting enough sleep, and engaging in activities that bring you joy and fulfillment.

Conclusion

Mindful aging is about embracing the aging process with grace, wisdom, and joy. By cultivating awareness and acceptance of the present moment, we can learn to navigate the ups and downs of aging with ease, and find meaning, purpose, and joy in the journey. Whether through mindfulness practices, physical activity, or simply appreciating the simple pleasures of life, we can learn to live fully in each moment, and make the most of the time we have. With mindfulness, we can age with grace, wisdom, and joy, finding peace and fulfillment in every stage of life.

18: Mindful Work: A Guide to Enhancing Your Career and Workplace Culture

Work is an integral part of our lives and it can significantly impact our well-being. The fast-paced and demanding nature of modern-day work can cause stress and burnout, leading to negative effects on our physical, emotional and mental health. However, incorporating mindfulness into the workplace can help to mitigate these negative effects and promote a healthier, happier and more productive work environment.

The first step in mindful work is to create a workplace culture that values and supports mindfulness. This can be achieved by promoting practices such as meditation, yoga, and mindful breathing, and encouraging employees to take breaks during the day to practice these techniques. Employers can also support their employees by creating a work environment that fosters a positive and supportive culture, where employees feel valued and respected.

Incorporating mindfulness into your workday can also help to improve your productivity and focus. By taking time to clear your mind and focus on the present moment, you can increase your clarity of thought and ability to tackle tasks with greater efficiency. Mindful communication can also improve relationships with coworkers and help to resolve conflicts, leading to a more harmonious workplace.

One of the key aspects of mindful work is to cultivate a positive and proactive attitude towards work. This means accepting challenges and responsibilities with an open mind, and focusing on finding solutions instead of dwelling on problems. By embracing this mindset, you can create a work environment that is fulfilling, fulfilling and purposeful.

Moreover, practicing mindfulness can also help to reduce stress and anxiety, allowing you to handle the demands of work with greater ease. This, in turn, can improve your physical and mental health, leading to a better work-life balance.

In conclusion, mindfulness can play a significant role in enhancing the work environment and promoting well-being. By creating a workplace culture that values and supports mindfulness, and incorporating mindful practices into your workday, you can improve your career, boost your productivity and live a more fulfilling and meaningful life.

19: The Importance of Self-Care and Mindful Self-compassion

Self-care is essential for maintaining a healthy body, mind, and spirit. It involves taking care of ourselves physically, emotionally, and mentally by engaging in activities that nourish and support our well-being. However, with the demands and pressures of daily life, it can be challenging to prioritize self-care and make it a regular part of our routine.

Mindful self-compassion is a critical aspect of self-care. It involves treating ourselves with kindness, understanding, and compassion, and recognizing that we are all human and susceptible to suffering and difficulties. By practicing self-compassion, we can create a positive and supportive inner dialogue, allowing us to be more resilient in the face of life's challenges.

One of the best ways to practice self-compassion is through mindfulness. Mindfulness helps us to be more present and aware in the moment, allowing us to observe our thoughts and emotions without judgment. This can help us to understand and accept our experiences, rather than resisting or avoiding them, and foster a sense of self-compassion.

19: THE IMPORTANCE OF SELF-CARE AND MINDFUL SELF-COMPASSION

Incorporating self-care practices into our daily routines can help to enhance our well-being and reduce stress and anxiety. Examples of self-care activities include getting regular exercise, eating a nutritious diet, getting enough sleep, and engaging in activities that bring joy and fulfillment. It is also essential to carve out time for self-reflection and introspection, as this can help us to better understand our thoughts and emotions, and promote a sense of inner peace.

Mindful self-compassion can also play a crucial role in promoting resilience and coping with life's challenges. By treating ourselves with kindness and understanding, we can develop a more positive and supportive inner dialogue, allowing us to bounce back from adversity more quickly. This can help to reduce feelings of stress, anxiety, and depression, leading to a more fulfilling and meaningful life.

In conclusion, self-care and mindful self-compassion are essential for maintaining a healthy body, mind, and spirit. By incorporating self-care practices into our daily routine and practicing self-compassion, we can enhance our well-being, reduce stress and anxiety, and live a more fulfilling and meaningful life.

20: Mindful Money: A Guide to Financial Well-being

Financial well-being is an essential aspect of overall well-being. It involves feeling secure, confident, and in control of our financial situation. However, money can often be a source of stress and anxiety, especially in today's fast-paced, consumer-driven society.

Mindful money is a concept that involves approaching our finances with awareness and purpose. It involves taking a holistic approach to money, recognizing that it is a tool that can help us achieve our goals and live a fulfilling life. By being mindful of our spending habits, savings goals, and investments, we can make informed financial decisions that align with our values and support our well-being.

One of the keys to mindful money is understanding our relationship with money. This involves reflecting on our beliefs, attitudes, and behaviors towards money, and recognizing how these impact our financial situation. By gaining insight into our relationship with money, we can develop a more positive and supportive mindset, allowing us to make informed financial decisions that support our well-being.

Another critical aspect of mindful money is creating a budget and spending plan. This involves determining our monthly income, expenses, and savings goals, and creating a plan to manage our money in a way that aligns with our values and supports our well-being. By creating a budget, we can gain control of our finances, reduce stress and anxiety, and work towards our financial goals.

Mindful money also involves investing in our financial education. This means learning about personal finance, financial planning, and investing, and developing the skills and knowledge needed to make informed financial decisions. This can help us to build wealth, reduce debt, and achieve our financial goals.

Incorporating mindfulness into our approach to money can help us to create a more fulfilling and meaningful relationship with our finances. By being present and intentional in our financial decisions, we can reduce stress and anxiety, achieve our financial goals, and live a more fulfilling life.

In conclusion, mindful money is a holistic approach to financial well-being that involves approaching our finances with awareness and purpose. By understanding our relationship with money, creating a budget, investing in our financial education, and being mindful of our spending habits, we can make informed financial decisions that support our well-being and lead to a more fulfilling life.

21: Mindful Travel: Exploring the World with Awareness and Presence

Travel is a wonderful opportunity to experience new cultures, meet new people, and explore the world. However, it can also be stressful, rushed, and disconnected from the present moment. Mindful travel is a way of approaching travel with awareness, presence, and intention, allowing us to fully immerse ourselves in our experiences and create meaningful memories.

One of the keys to mindful travel is slowing down and being present. This means avoiding the urge to rush from one place to the next, and instead taking the time to fully experience each moment. This could involve spending time exploring a local market, chatting with locals, or simply taking a walk and soaking up the sights, sounds, and smells of a new place.

Another important aspect of mindful travel is connecting with local cultures. This involves seeking out authentic experiences, learning about local traditions and customs, and engaging with local communities. By connecting with local cultures, we can gain a deeper understanding of the world, and create more meaningful and fulfilling travel experiences.

Mindful travel also involves being mindful of our impact on the environment. This means taking steps to reduce our carbon footprint, being mindful of our waste and consumption, and choosing sustainable travel options where possible. By being mindful of our impact on the environment, we can ensure that our travel experiences are in harmony with the natural world.

Incorporating mindfulness into our approach to travel can help us to create more meaningful and fulfilling experiences. By slowing down, connecting with local cultures, and being mindful of our impact on the environment, we can fully immerse ourselves in our travel experiences and create memories that will last a lifetime.

In conclusion, mindful travel is a way of approaching travel with awareness, presence, and intention. By slowing down, connecting with local cultures, and being mindful of our impact on the environment, we can create more meaningful and fulfilling travel experiences that allow us to fully immerse ourselves in the world and create memories that will last a lifetime.

22: Mindful Sexuality: Enhancing Intimacy and Relationships

Sexuality is an important aspect of our lives and can have a significant impact on our physical, emotional, and psychological well-being. Mindful sexuality is a way of approaching sexuality with awareness, presence, and intention, allowing us to deepen our connections with ourselves and our partners, and enhance our overall sexual experiences.

One of the keys to mindful sexuality is being aware of our thoughts and feelings. This means paying attention to our thoughts, feelings, and sensations during sexual experiences, and being mindful of any emotions that arise. By being aware of our thoughts and feelings, we can increase our self-awareness and understand how our experiences are affecting us.

Another important aspect of mindful sexuality is communication. This involves open, honest, and respectful communication with our partners, and taking the time to listen and understand each other's needs, desires, and boundaries. Communication is key to developing healthy and fulfilling sexual relationships, and can help us to avoid misunderstandings, conflicts, and negative experiences.

22: MINDFUL SEXUALITY: ENHANCING INTIMACY AND RELATIONSHIPS

Mindful sexuality also involves being present and focused during sexual experiences. This means avoiding distractions, such as phones, and focusing on the sensations, feelings, and experiences of the moment. By being present and focused during sexual experiences, we can deepen our connections with ourselves and our partners, and enhance our overall sexual experiences.

Incorporating mindfulness into our approach to sexuality can help us to develop deeper connections with ourselves and our partners, and enhance our overall sexual experiences. By being aware of our thoughts and feelings, communicating openly and respectfully, and being present and focused during sexual experiences, we can deepen our understanding of ourselves, our partners, and the world around us, and create more meaningful and fulfilling sexual experiences.

In conclusion, mindful sexuality is a way of approaching sexuality with awareness, presence, and intention. By being aware of our thoughts and feelings, communicating openly and respectfully, and being present and focused during sexual experiences, we can deepen our connections with ourselves and our partners, and enhance our overall sexual experiences, leading to a more fulfilling and meaningful life.

23: Mindful Creativity: Unlocking Your Inner Artist

Creativity is an essential aspect of human life and is often considered the driving force behind innovation and progress. However, in our fast-paced, technology-driven world, it's easy to lose touch with our creative side. Stress and anxiety can also limit our ability to think creatively and enjoy life to the fullest. Mindfulness can help you to reclaim your creativity and tap into your inner artist.

What is Mindful Creativity?

Mindful creativity is the practice of bringing awareness and presence to the creative process. It is about letting go of judgment and embracing your unique perspective and ideas. This approach encourages you to let go of expectations and simply enjoy the process of creating. When you are mindful in your creative pursuits, you allow yourself to experience the joy of the present moment, connecting with your inner artist and allowing your creative ideas to flow.

Benefits of Mindful Creativity

There are many benefits to incorporating mindfulness into

your creative practice. Here are a few of the most significant benefits:

– Improved Focus and Concentration: By practicing mindfulness, you can cultivate focus and concentration, which are essential for creativity.

– Enhanced Self-Awareness: Mindfulness helps you to be more self-aware and understand your own thought processes and emotions, which can improve your creativity.

– Increased Confidence: When you practice mindfulness, you can develop greater self-confidence, which can lead to an increase in creative output.

– Reduces Stress and Anxiety: Mindfulness is an effective tool for reducing stress and anxiety, which can limit creativity. By practicing mindfulness, you can create a more relaxed state of mind, which can enhance your creative abilities.

Tips for Mindful Creativity

Here are some tips for incorporating mindfulness into your creative practice:

23: MINDFUL CREATIVITY: UNLOCKING YOUR INNER ARTIST

– Set aside time: Set aside specific time in your day to focus on your creative pursuits. Whether it's drawing, painting, writing or playing an instrument, be intentional about the time you dedicate to your creative practice.

– Start Small: Don't feel like you have to create a masterpiece every time you sit down to create. Start small and focus on the process, rather than the end product.

– Let go of expectations: Be gentle with yourself and let go of any expectations or judgments. Allow yourself to simply enjoy the process of creating.

– Focus on the present moment: When you're creating, focus on the present moment. Pay attention to the sensations in your body, the sounds around you, and the emotions you experience as you create.

– Practice gratitude: Take a moment before and after your creative practice to reflect on what you're grateful for and the joy of the creative process.

In conclusion, mindfulness can be a powerful tool for enhancing creativity and unlocking your inner artist. By incorporating mindfulness into your creative pursuits, you can experience the joy of the present moment and tap into your creative potential. Remember, creativity is not about perfection, but rather about the process and the joy of expressing yourself. So, let go of expectations and embrace the power of mindful creativity.

24: Mindful Education: Transforming Learning and Teaching

Education is an integral part of our lives, and it has the power to shape our futures and impact our well-being. But, traditional education systems often focus on academic performance, rather than the development of personal skills and emotional intelligence. Mindful education aims to address this imbalance, incorporating mindfulness practices into learning environments to support students in becoming more self-aware, compassionate, and resilient.

One of the main benefits of mindful education is that it helps students develop emotional intelligence, which is essential for success in both personal and professional life. By practicing mindfulness, students can better understand their own emotions and those of others, leading to improved communication skills, stronger relationships, and increased empathy.

Mindful education also encourages students to develop a growth mindset, where they see challenges as opportunities for growth and learning, rather than setbacks. This type of mindset is crucial for success in life, as it helps individuals to approach challenges with a positive attitude and the belief that they can improve with effort.

For teachers, mindfulness practices can help reduce stress and increase job satisfaction. By incorporating mindfulness into the classroom, teachers can create a more positive learning environment and improve their own well-being, while also promoting the same benefits in their students.

Mindful education is not just limited to schools, it can also be applied in colleges, universities, and even professional training programs. By integrating mindfulness practices into educational settings, students can develop life-long skills that will benefit them both personally and professionally.

In conclusion, mindful education is a transformative approach to learning and teaching that can help students develop emotional intelligence, a growth mindset, and the skills to live a fulfilling life. By incorporating mindfulness into the education system, we can create a generation of individuals who are well-rounded, compassionate, and resilient.

25: Mindful Activism: Creating Positive Change with Awareness and Compassion

Mindfulness is not only a way to improve one's own well-being, but it can also be a powerful tool for creating positive change in the world. In this chapter, we will explore the concept of mindful activism and how it can be used to bring about positive change in a compassionate and non-violent way.

Mindful activism involves using mindfulness practices and principles to engage in activism and social justice work. This means approaching activism with an open and non-judgmental mind, and being fully present in the moment to understand the issues and perspectives of all those involved. By doing so, mindful activists are able to approach activism with greater empathy, clarity, and effectiveness.

One key aspect of mindful activism is being mindful of one's own thoughts, feelings, and reactions. This can help activists avoid getting caught up in negative emotions and reactions, and instead stay centered and focused on the issue at hand. Mindful activism also involves taking time to reflect on one's actions and the impact they may have on others, as well as being mindful of the effects of one's activism on the environment and other living beings.

Another important aspect of mindful activism is being mindful of the power dynamics at play in any given situation. This means being aware of one's own privilege and how it may impact one's activism, as well as being mindful of how oppression and marginalization may impact those who are being impacted by the issue at hand. Mindful activists strive to create a more equitable and just world, and being mindful of power dynamics is an important part of this work.

There are many different forms of activism that can be approached with mindfulness, including environmental activism, animal rights activism, human rights activism, and more. Regardless of the specific issue, mindful activism always involves approaching activism with compassion, nonviolence, and a deep understanding of the perspectives and experiences of all those involved.

In conclusion, mindful activism is an important way to create positive change in the world and bring about a more just and equitable society. By approaching activism with mindfulness, compassion, and a deep understanding of the issues and perspectives involved, activists can be more effective in their work and bring about lasting change in a peaceful and non-violent way.

26: Mindful Community Building: Connecting with Others for a Better World

Building a strong and supportive community is an essential aspect of a fulfilling life. By connecting with others and sharing our experiences, we can create a sense of belonging and deepen our sense of purpose. Mindful community building is the process of cultivating awareness, compassion, and connection in our relationships with others.

In this chapter, we will explore how mindfulness can be used to enhance our relationships with others and build stronger communities. We will also discuss the benefits of mindfulness for community building, such as increased empathy, improved communication, and greater sense of belonging.

Benefits of Mindful Community Building

Mindful community building has a positive impact on our well-being in several ways. Firstly, it helps to increase our sense of empathy and understanding for others, which can lead to more positive relationships. When we are mindful in our interactions with others, we are more likely to listen deeply, understand their perspectives, and respond with compassion.

In addition, mindfulness can improve our communication skills, making it easier to build meaningful relationships. When we are present in the moment, we can listen more deeply, express ourselves more clearly, and avoid misunder-standings. As a result, our relationships become more au-thentic, meaningful, and fulfilling.

Another benefit of mindful community building is a greater sense of belonging. When we connect with others in a mind-ful way, we feel a deeper sense of connection to our com-munity, which can increase our sense of well-being. This sense of belonging can help us feel more grounded, secure, and content in our lives.

How to Practice Mindful Community Building

– Be Present: When interacting with others, try to be fully present in the moment. Avoid distractions, such as checking your phone or thinking about other things, and focus on the person you are speaking with.

26: MINDFUL COMMUNITY BUILDING: CONNECTING WITH OTHERS FOR A BETTER WORLD

– Listen Deeply: Pay attention to the other person's words, body language, and emotions. Try to understand their perspective and respond with empathy and compassion.

– Practice Active Listening: Repeat back what the other person has said to show that you are listening and to clarify any misunderstandings.

– Be Authentic: Be true to yourself and express your thoughts and feelings in an honest and open way. This can deepen your relationships and build trust.

– Cultivate Gratitude: Express gratitude for the people in your life and acknowledge their positive qualities. This can enhance your relationships and build a positive community atmosphere.

– Get Involved: Participate in community events and activities to build relationships and a sense of belonging.

In conclusion, mindful community building is an important aspect of well-being that can enhance our relationships, improve our communication skills, and deepen our sense of belonging. By practicing mindfulness and compassion in our interactions with others, we can build stronger and more meaningful relationships, which will benefit both ourselves and our communities.

27: Mindful Entrepreneurship: Building Success with Purpose and Passion

Entrepreneurship is a challenging journey that requires focus, dedication, and resilience. But with the right mindset and approach, it can also be one of the most rewarding experiences of your life. In this chapter, we'll explore how mindfulness can help you build a successful business with purpose and passion.

First, let's start with a definition of mindfulness. Mindfulness is the practice of being present and aware in the moment, without judgment. It's about accepting things as they are, without trying to change them. This state of awareness can bring a sense of calm and peace, and it can also help you make better decisions, build stronger relationships, and find more joy and meaning in your life.

So, how does mindfulness apply to entrepreneurship? Entrepreneurship is about creating something new and valuable, and it often involves a lot of uncertainty, risk, and stress. Mindfulness can help you navigate these challenges by providing you with a sense of clarity and focus. It can also help you maintain a positive outlook, even in the face of adversity.

Here are some of the ways that mindfulness can benefit entrepreneurs:

– Clarity of Purpose: Mindfulness can help you clarify your vision and purpose, and stay focused on what's truly important. When you're mindful, you're able to see the big picture, and you're better able to prioritize your actions and make informed decisions.

– Resilience: Entrepreneurship can be a rollercoaster ride, with many ups and downs. Mindfulness can help you develop resilience, so you're better able to handle the stress and uncertainty that comes with building a business.

– Better Decision Making: Mindfulness can help you make better decisions by providing you with a sense of clarity and focus. When you're mindful, you're better able to see the consequences of your actions, and you're more likely to make decisions that align with your values and goals.

– Stronger Relationships: Mindfulness can help you build

stronger relationships with your team, partners, and customers. When you're mindful, you're better able to communicate effectively, and you're more likely to build trust and respect with others.

– Increased Productivity: Mindfulness can help you increase your productivity by reducing stress and improving your focus. When you're mindful, you're better able to prioritize your actions and stay focused on what's truly important.

To incorporate mindfulness into your entrepreneurial journey, start by setting aside a few minutes each day for meditation or mindfulness practice. You can also try incorporating mindfulness into your work routine, by taking breaks to focus on your breathing or by taking a mindful walk in nature.

In conclusion, mindfulness can be a powerful tool for entrepreneurs, helping them build successful businesses with purpose and passion. By incorporating mindfulness into your daily routine, you can increase your clarity of purpose, resilience, better decision making, stronger relationships, and productivity. So start your mindful entrepreneurial journey today and unlock the power of presence in your work and life!

28: Mindful Athletics: Enhancing Performance and Well-being through Awareness

Athletics is a demanding and competitive field that requires not only physical strength and skill, but also mental resilience and focus. Mindfulness practices can be an effective way to help athletes develop these essential qualities and enhance their overall performance and well-being.

One of the key benefits of mindfulness for athletes is improved focus and concentration. When we are mindful, we bring our full attention to the present moment, rather than being distracted by worries about the future or regrets about the past. This heightened level of focus can help athletes perform at their best, by reducing distractions and allowing them to remain fully engaged in the game or competition.

Mindfulness can also help athletes manage stress and anxiety, which can often arise in high-pressure situations. By developing a calm and clear mind, athletes can better handle the pressure and remain focused on the task at hand. This can help to reduce performance anxiety and improve overall mental toughness.

In addition to these performance benefits, mindfulness can also improve overall well-being and quality of life for athletes. Regular mindfulness practice has been shown to reduce symptoms of depression and anxiety, boost immune function, and improve sleep quality. This can help athletes to maintain a positive outlook, even in the face of setbacks and challenges.

To incorporate mindfulness into your athletic practice, start by setting aside a few minutes each day for meditation or deep breathing exercises. As you become more comfortable with these practices, you can begin to incorporate mindfulness into your athletic routines, such as by focusing on your breath during warm-up exercises or taking a moment to pause and reflect before a game.

Finally, remember that mindfulness is a lifelong journey, and it takes time and dedication to see the full benefits. Be patient with yourself, and remember that progress, not perfection, is the goal. With consistent practice, you will develop the mental resilience and focus you need to take your athletic performance to the next level and achieve greater well-being and happiness.

29: Mindful Technology: Balancing the Digital World with Inner Peace

In today's fast-paced world, technology plays a major role in our daily lives. From smartphones to laptops and everything in between, it's hard to imagine life without these digital devices. However, despite their convenience, technology can also have negative impacts on our mental and physical health, leading to stress, anxiety, and even addiction.

Incorporating mindfulness into our relationship with technology can help balance its impact on our well-being. By being more aware and intentional about our use of technology, we can use it to support rather than hinder our health and happiness.

Here are some tips for incorporating mindfulness into your relationship with technology:

– Set Limits: Establishing boundaries around your use of technology is important to maintain balance. Consider setting aside specific times each day to check your devices, and make a commitment to disconnect during designated "screen-free" periods.

29: MINDFUL TECHNOLOGY: BALANCING THE DIGITAL WORLD WITH INNER PEACE

– Be Present: When using technology, practice being present and fully engaged with what you're doing. Avoid multitasking or mindlessly scrolling through social media, and instead focus on the task at hand.

– Connect with the Natural World: Spending time in nature can be a powerful way to reduce stress and increase well-being. Try disconnecting from your devices and connecting with the natural world through activities such as hiking, gardening, or simply spending time outdoors.

– Use Mindful Apps: There are a number of apps designed to help you practice mindfulness and manage technology use. These can include guided meditations, screen time tracking, and mindfulness reminders.

– Be Intentional: Make a conscious effort to be intentional about how you use technology. Rather than being reactive, decide ahead of time how you want to use your devices and be mindful of the impact they have on your well-being.

Incorporating mindfulness into your relationship with technology can help you balance its impact on your well-being and use it in a way that supports your health and happiness.

29: MINDFUL TECHNOLOGY: BALANCING THE DIGITAL WORLD WITH INNER PEACE

By being more intentional and aware of your use of technology, you can use it to enhance rather than hinder your life.

30: Mindful Spirituality: Connecting with a Higher Power for Inner Peace

Spirituality and mindfulness are often intertwined, as both seek to provide a deeper understanding of the self and the world around us. The practice of mindfulness can be seen as a spiritual path in and of itself, but for many, it is also a way to connect with a higher power or divine force.

The concept of spirituality varies greatly from person to person, with some connecting through organized religion, while others find solace in nature, art, or other forms of self-expression. Whatever form it takes, spirituality can provide a sense of purpose, meaning, and connection that contributes to our overall well-being.

When combined with mindfulness, spirituality can offer a rich and fulfilling experience, as we become more attuned to the present moment and our inner selves. This awareness can deepen our connection with a higher power and help us to find peace and comfort in difficult times.

Incorporating mindfulness into spiritual practices, such as prayer, meditation, or rituals, can help us to focus on the present moment and connect more deeply with the divine. Whether we turn to a particular religious tradition or simply seek a deeper connection with the universe, mindfulness can help us to tap into the inner peace and joy that spirituality can bring.

Moreover, practicing mindfulness can also help us to overcome feelings of anxiety, fear, or anger that may arise in spiritual experiences. By learning to observe our thoughts and emotions without judgment, we can approach spiritual moments with more equanimity and compassion, and connect with the divine in a more meaningful and enriching way.

In this chapter, we will explore the connection between mindfulness and spirituality and discuss ways to cultivate a mindful spiritual practice that can enrich our lives and bring us inner peace. Whether you are a seasoned spiritual practitioner or just starting out, this chapter will provide you with tools and insights to help you connect with your inner selves and the divine in a deeper, more fulfilling way.

31: Mindful Aging: Embracing the Journey with Grace and Wisdom

As we age, it can be easy to feel overwhelmed by the changes and challenges that come with growing older. However, aging is an opportunity to deepen our understanding of ourselves and the world around us, and to cultivate a sense of inner peace and fulfillment. By embracing the journey with grace and wisdom, we can live our later years with purpose, meaning, and joy.

Mindfulness is a powerful tool for navigating the challenges of aging, helping us to stay present in each moment and to cultivate a sense of inner peace and contentment. By focusing on the present moment and accepting the reality of our experiences, we can develop a more positive and accepting attitude towards aging and find meaning in the journey.

One of the key benefits of mindfulness for aging is the way it helps us to cultivate a sense of self-compassion. As we age, it can be easy to become overly critical of ourselves, leading to feelings of anxiety, stress, and low self-esteem. By practicing self-compassion, we can learn to accept ourselves and our experiences, and to be kind and compassionate towards ourselves as we navigate the ups and downs of aging.

Mindfulness can also help us to stay connected to our inner selves and to the world around us. As we age, it can be easy to feel isolated and disconnected from others, but mindfulness practices like meditation, yoga, and tai chi can help us to stay engaged with the world and to connect with others in meaningful ways.

In addition to these benefits, mindfulness can also help us to find meaning and purpose in our later years. Whether through volunteering, pursuing hobbies and interests, or spending time with loved ones, mindfulness can help us to stay engaged with the world and to find joy and fulfillment in our later years.

Ultimately, aging is a journey that we can embrace with grace and wisdom, and mindfulness is a powerful tool for helping us to stay present and connected to ourselves, others, and the world around us. By embracing the journey with mindfulness and self-compassion, we can find joy, meaning, and purpose in our later years, and live a life of inner peace and fulfillment.

32: Mindful Healing: Using Mindfulness to Overcome Physical and Emotional Pain

Mindfulness can play a significant role in helping us cope with physical and emotional pain. When we are mindful, we bring awareness and attention to our experience in the present moment, which can help us manage and reduce pain. In this chapter, we will explore the connection between mindfulness and healing and how it can help us overcome physical and emotional pain.

Physical pain is a common experience that affects many people. Whether it's chronic pain caused by an underlying condition or acute pain from an injury, it can be debilitating and interfere with daily activities. Conventional treatments, such as medication and physical therapy, can help alleviate pain, but they do not address the underlying psychological and emotional components. Mindfulness, on the other hand, has been shown to help reduce chronic pain by addressing these components.

Studies have shown that mindfulness can help reduce chronic pain by decreasing stress and anxiety, which can amplify pain. By paying attention to the present moment, we can better understand our pain and develop a greater sense of control over it. Mindful breathing, meditation, and body scan techniques can also help us stay focused on the present moment, reducing the impact of pain on our lives.

Emotional pain, such as anxiety and depression, can be just as debilitating as physical pain. However, it can be more challenging to manage because it often involves complex thoughts and feelings that are difficult to understand and process. Mindfulness can help us deal with emotional pain by helping us develop self-compassion and reducing the impact of negative thoughts and emotions.

Through mindfulness, we can learn to accept our emotions, rather than fighting against them. By paying attention to our thoughts and feelings, we can better understand the root causes of our emotional pain and develop a greater sense of control over it. Mindful self-compassion and positive affirmations can also help us cultivate a more positive outlook on life and reduce the impact of negative thoughts and emotions.

In conclusion, mindfulness can play an important role in

healing both physical and emotional pain. By bringing awareness and attention to the present moment, we can better understand and manage our pain, reducing its impact on our lives. Whether you are dealing with physical or emotional pain, incorporating mindfulness into your daily life can help you achieve greater well-being and inner peace.

33: Mindful Grief: Navigating Loss with Compassion and Understanding

Grief is a natural and inevitable part of life that affects us all in one way or another. It can come in the form of the loss of a loved one, a pet, a job, a relationship, or even a life transition. Regardless of the cause, grief can be an extremely difficult and challenging experience. It can bring feelings of sadness, anger, guilt, loneliness, and confusion.

In traditional Western societies, grief is often viewed as something to be overcome and pushed aside as quickly as possible. However, this approach can lead to incomplete healing and even long-term psychological problems. Mindfulness offers an alternative way of dealing with grief by providing us with a set of tools to navigate our emotions and thoughts in a more compassionate and accepting way.

Mindful grief can help us to find peace and acceptance in the midst of our pain. By using mindfulness to focus on the present moment and to be more aware of our thoughts and emotions, we can develop a more accepting and compassionate relationship with our grief. This can allow us to fully experience our emotions and work through them in a healthy and constructive way.

There are several mindfulness techniques that can be particularly helpful in dealing with grief. One such technique is mindful breathing. By focusing on our breath and allowing ourselves to be fully present in the moment, we can reduce stress and anxiety and find a sense of calm. Another technique is mindful visualization, where we imagine ourselves in a peaceful and supportive environment, such as a beach or a forest. This can help us to release negative emotions and to develop a more positive outlook on life.

In addition to mindfulness techniques, there are also several strategies for dealing with grief that are rooted in mindfulness principles. One such strategy is to cultivate gratitude and positive thinking. By focusing on what we are grateful for, we can shift our attention away from our pain and find a sense of joy and happiness in life. Another strategy is to practice self-compassion. By being kind and understanding with ourselves, we can reduce self-blame and negative self-talk, and develop a more positive and supportive relationship with ourselves.

In conclusion, mindfulness can be a valuable tool in dealing with grief. By using mindfulness to be more aware of our thoughts and emotions, and to cultivate compassion and positivity, we can navigate our grief in a more peaceful and accepting way. As we work through our grief, we can find a sense of inner peace and resilience that can support us in the future.

34: Mindful Mental Health: Overcoming Depression and Anxiety through Awareness

Mental health is a crucial aspect of overall well-being and mindfulness has been shown to have a profound impact on our emotional and psychological health. In this chapter, we will explore the connection between mindfulness and mental health, and how it can be used to overcome depression and anxiety.

Depression and anxiety are two of the most common mental health issues faced by people today. They can significantly impact a person's quality of life and cause physical, emotional and psychological distress. In many cases, conventional treatments such as medication and therapy may not be effective or may have limited results. However, mindfulness can provide an alternative approach to managing these conditions and lead to significant improvements in mental health.

Mindfulness has been shown to increase resilience and improve mood by reducing negative thoughts and emotions. It also helps individuals to be more self-aware and to understand their thoughts and emotions in a more holistic and compassionate way. This, in turn, allows them to better manage their thoughts and emotions and to have a more positive and healthier outlook on life.

To begin using mindfulness to overcome depression and anxiety, it's important to understand the fundamental principles of mindfulness. Mindfulness is the practice of being present and attentive to the moment, without judgment or distraction. This can be achieved through various practices such as mindfulness meditation, mindful breathing, and mindful movement.

Mindfulness meditation is one of the most effective techniques for managing depression and anxiety. It involves focusing on the present moment and paying attention to your thoughts and emotions without judgment. This can help to reduce negative thoughts and increase feelings of peace and calm.

Another mindfulness practice that can help to manage depression and anxiety is mindful breathing. This involves taking slow, deep breaths and focusing on the sensation of breathing in and out. This technique can help to slow down the mind and reduce feelings of stress and anxiety.

Mindful movement, such as yoga and tai chi, is another effective way to use mindfulness to overcome depression and
anxiety. These practices involve moving slowly and mindfully, paying close attention to your body and breathing.
This helps to reduce tension and increase feelings of relaxation and peace.

In conclusion, mindfulness has the potential to be a powerful tool in the management of depression and anxiety. It
helps individuals to understand their thoughts and emotions in a more holistic and compassionate way, leading to
improved mental health and overall well-being. To get started with mindfulness, it's important to understand the fundamental principles and to incorporate mindfulness practices into your daily routine. By doing so, you can begin to
experience the benefits of mindfulness and overcome depression and anxiety.

35: Mindful Recovery: Using Mindfulness to Overcome Addictions and Habits

Addiction and habits can take a heavy toll on our physical and mental health. Whether it's drugs, alcohol, gambling, shopping, or any other substance or behavior, addiction can be a difficult cycle to break. However, with the help of mindfulness, it is possible to overcome these negative patterns and cultivate healthier habits for a happier, more fulfilling life.

What is Mindful Recovery?

Mindful recovery is a holistic approach to overcoming addiction that combines mindfulness with traditional recovery methods. It focuses on developing self-awareness, compassion, and positive habits through the practice of mindfulness. By becoming more aware of our thoughts, feelings, and behaviors, we can learn to identify the triggers that lead to addictive behavior and make better decisions for our well-being.

The Benefits of Mindful Recovery

35: MINDFUL RECOVERY: USING MINDFULNESS TO OVERCOME ADDICTIONS AND HABITS

– Increased Self-Awareness: Mindful recovery helps individuals gain a deeper understanding of their thoughts, feelings, and behaviors. This increased self-awareness can help individuals identify the root causes of their addictive behavior and develop a more effective plan for recovery.

– Better Coping Skills: By practicing mindfulness, individuals can learn to manage their emotions and thoughts in a healthier way. This helps them better cope with stress, anxiety, and other triggers that may lead to addictive behavior.

– Improved Mental Health: Research has shown that mindfulness can help reduce symptoms of anxiety, depression, and other mental health conditions. By incorporating mindfulness into recovery, individuals can improve their overall mental health and well-being.

– Increased Willpower: Mindfulness helps individuals cultivate more willpower and discipline, which can be particularly helpful in overcoming addiction. By developing a strong, centered mind, individuals can make better decisions and resist temptations that may trigger addictive behavior.

35: MINDFUL RECOVERY: USING MINDFULNESS TO OVERCOME ADDICTIONS AND HABITS

– Stronger Support System: Mindful recovery encourages individuals to connect with others in their recovery journey. This can help build a strong support system, which is crucial for long-term success in overcoming addiction.

Mindful Recovery Techniques

– Mindful Breathing: Mindful breathing is a simple but powerful technique for reducing stress and calming the mind. It involves focusing on the breath and letting go of distracting thoughts. This can be particularly helpful in managing cravings and triggers.

– Mindful Meditation: Mindful meditation helps individuals focus their attention on the present moment, reducing stress and anxiety. It can also help individuals develop greater self-awareness and improve mental well-being.

– Body Scan: The body scan technique involves lying down and focusing on each part of the body, noticing sensations and releasing tension. This can be particularly helpful in reducing stress and improving relaxation.

– Yoga: Yoga is a physical and mental practice that can help individuals improve their physical and mental well-being. By combining physical postures with mindfulness, yoga can help reduce stress, increase flexibility, and improve overall health.

– Gratitude Practice: A gratitude practice involves taking time each day to reflect on things that you are grateful for. This can help shift your focus from negative patterns and improve your overall outlook on life.

Final Thoughts

Mindful recovery is a powerful tool for overcoming addiction and cultivating healthier habits. By becoming more self-aware, developing coping skills, and improving mental health, individuals can achieve long-term success in their recovery journey. Remember that recovery is a lifelong process, and it's important to seek support from loved ones, a therapist, or a recovery program when needed. With patience, dedication, and the right tools, anyone can overcome addiction and cultivate a happier, more fulfilling life.

36: Conclusion: Living a Life of Mindful Well-being and Inner Peace

The practice of mindfulness is a journey, not a destination. As you embark on this journey, you may encounter challenges and obstacles along the way. However, with persistence and dedication, you can overcome these obstacles and experience a greater sense of well-being and inner peace. The benefits of mindfulness are numerous and far-reaching, affecting every aspect of our lives, from our physical health to our relationships and careers. Whether you are seeking to improve your mental and emotional health, develop stronger relationships, or enhance your overall well-being, mindfulness has the power to transform your life.

One of the most important things to remember about mindfulness is that it is a lifelong practice. It requires effort and dedication, but the rewards are well worth the effort. With time, patience, and perseverance, you will begin to see changes in your thoughts, emotions, and behaviors. As you become more aware of your thoughts and emotions, you will develop a greater understanding of yourself and others. This increased self-awareness will lead to a greater sense of compassion and empathy, which in turn will strengthen your relationships with others.

Incorporating mindfulness into your daily life can help you overcome stress and anxiety, improve your physical and mental health, and enhance your relationships and career. Whether you are practicing mindful breathing, mindful movement, or mindful communication, the key is to be present in the moment, without judgment. By cultivating this awareness, you will gain a deeper understanding of yourself and others, and begin to experience a greater sense of inner peace and well-being.

In conclusion, mindfulness is a powerful tool that can help you transform your life. Whether you are seeking to improve your mental and emotional health, develop stronger relationships, or enhance your overall well-being, the practice of mindfulness has the power to bring positive change into your life. So, take a deep breath, let go of any expectations or judgments, and embrace this journey of mindfulness and well-being. With time and dedication, you will begin to experience a greater sense of peace, joy, and fulfillment in your life.

Thank You

As we reach the end of this book, I want to say thanks for reading this book.

I want to get this information out to as many people as possible. If you found this book helpful, I would greatly appreciate you leaving me a review. This helps others find the book as well.

Disclaimer

This document is geared towards providing exact and reliable information in regards to the topic and issue covered. The publication is sold on the idea that the publisher is not required to render an accounting, officially permitted, or otherwise, qualified services. If advice is necessary, legal, financial, medical or professional, a practiced individual in the profession should be ordered.

This information is not presented by a financial or medical practitioner and is for entertainment, educational and informational purposes only. The content is not intended as a substitute for professional medical advice, diagnosis, or treatment. Always seek the advice of your physician or other qualified health care provider with any questions you may have regarding a medical condition. Never disregard professional medical advice or delay in seeking it because of something you have read.

The information provided herein is stated to be truthful and consistent, in that any liability, in terms of inattention or otherwise, by any usage or abuse of any policies, processes, or directions contained within is the solitary and utter responsibility of the recipient reader. Under no circumstances

DISCLAIMER

will any legal responsibility or blame be held against the publisher for any reparation, damages, or monetary loss due to the information herein, either directly or indirectly.

www.ingramcontent.com/pod-product-compliance
Lightning Source LLC
Chambersburg PA
CBHW060323130626
46553CB00003B/895